FANTASTIC BEASTS AND WHERE TO FIND THEM

SWOOPING EVIL

AN INSIDE LOOK AT MAGIZOOLOGY IN THE FILM

BY JODY REVENSON

A Division of Insight Editions, LP
San Rafael, California

INTRODUCTION

It's the year 1926 and Magizoologist Newt Scamander, a wizard who studies magical creatures, has come to the United States after a year of traveling. He says he's visiting New York City because he's heard that breeders of the rare Appaloosa Puffskein live there, and he wants to pick one up for a friend. Newt has already found many fantastic beasts during his adventures around the globe, and he keeps and cares for a number of them in what appears to be a normal-size leather case (but is actually magically expanded, of course). Unfortunately, soon after his arrival in New York City, some of the creatures escape and Newt must track them down. So begins a new story set in J.K. Rowling's wizarding world: *Fantastic Beasts and Where to Find Them*. During his search, he finds help and forms new friendships with Americans Jacob Kowalski and Tina and Queenie Goldstein.

NEWT SCAMANDER

Actor Eddie Redmayne, who plays Newt Scamander, describes the Magizoologist as someone who feels more at home with creatures than he does with other wizards. "He's a passionate fellow, which I love about him," he says, "and he's got an agenda." The beasts of the wizarding world are primarily feared in the United States, Eddie explains. They're seen as a threat, because they might give away the existence of wizards to No-Majs (the US equivalent of Muggles, or non-magical people). Newt believes that if the wizarding community were properly educated about them, "they could learn to live side by side, and appreciate how extraordinary [these magical beasts] are."

Director David Yates continues, "Newt is a bit of an outsider, though there's something really sweet about him. He's unique in that he's one of the few wizards who believe that these creatures should be cherished. Everyone else thinks he's nuts, because they're dangerous, scary things." Eddie was drawn into the story by the interaction between Newt and his creatures. "Not only did J.K. Rowling create individual beasts with character," he says, "but also with specific relationships with Newt." Even though the creatures were computer-generated, Eddie always kept their individual personalities in mind during filming. Lending a hand was a team of puppeteers who created representations of the creatures to provide proper eye lines and means for interaction for the actors. The animation director, Pablo Grillo, even helped Eddie in a scene by acting out the Niffler's part!

Adventurous Attire

Newt Scamander's beautiful peacock-blue coat makes more than just a fashion statement. Although Newt essentially wears one outfit throughout the film, costume designer Colleen Atwood made subtle changes to his clothing as the story progressed to show changes in Newt himself. As Eddie explains, "The collar pops up, and the trousers go into his boots, for example. There's an eccentric, nerdy quality to him at the start, but it becomes the look of an adventurer by the end of the film."

NEWT'S CASE

Newt Scamander goes beyond just studying creatures; he collects and rehabilitates rare, endangered, and exotic beasts, and keeps them in a case where each is provided with its own unique environment that has been magically created. Actor Dan Fogler, who plays No-Maj Jacob Kowalski, was in as much awe of the environments inside the case as his character: "Inside the case are all these different floating landscapes. There's a snowy tundra and one with rolling fields. There's a savannah and a bamboo forest. It's like a multidimensional wildlife park, and for the production team to make this happen was its own form of magic." The case's interior was a mixture of practical and digital sets, which production designer Stuart Craig refers to as "magical extensions."

A World Within a World

"Newt's case is his world," says actor Eddie Redmayne. "It's his haven, really. And the set Stuart built was everything I could have dreamed of and more." Eddie feels that the interior of the case is a reflection of Newt's character. "There's an almost biological element to it," he explains. "You see the passion he has for these different animals and plants. You see the drawings he's done. It really was his character in physical terms, in a way. And once you descend into his shed and then out into the world of the case, well, it really pushes imagination to new extremes."

WELCOME TO NEW YORK

Newt arrives at the Port Authority of New York, where his baggage will be inspected. Newt has obviously thought ahead about this, and so his case has a special lock that can shift to become "Muggle Worthy." When it is opened by the customs official, it reveals a tourist's necessities: a map of New York, an alarm clock, and binoculars—and additionally for Newt, a magnifying glass and his Hufflepuff scarf. While Newt flips the lock to "Muggle Worthy" in the film, the "lock" was actually operated by remote control during shooting. Several cases were created for different uses, including one with a false bottom in addition to the Muggle Worthy version.

Fantastic Environments

Production designer Stuart Craig and concept artist Dermot Power considered many ideas for the creatures' habitats inside Newt's case. "We talked about cabinets with dioramas, and possibly a Victorian-type museum," Stuart recalls, "but those wouldn't do for live animals." Zoos were a

a comment she made, which was that Newt's not that good a wizard!"

The environments Newt has put together for his creatures are more than adequate and quite a bit imperfect. "My impression is that Newt just loves animals," says Dermot, "and he loves them

closer feel, but Stuart knew that Newt would not keep his creatures in cages. "Newt is about the preservation of these creatures," says Stuart, "and their happiness in their respective environments. He would have made these magical environments himself." The next idea was to re-create each creature's original habitat. "So when you stepped into the Erumpent environment, for example," says concept artist Dermot Power, "it would feel like its natural terrain." This design was shown to J.K. Rowling, who described it as "too epic." It was easy enough to scale back, but the team still wanted to address Newt's personal construction of the habitats. "And the key thing that unlocked the design direction for us," Dermot continues, "was

so much he's gone to great trouble to create these worlds for them, but I imagine that he doesn't see his career as being the greatest world-creator. He's done the most beautiful worlds *he* can do. And though they're a bit shaky, he makes sure they still work." Newt has also created painterly backdrops that surround the environments. "He's trying to fool the creatures, but then, he's not trying too hard," Dermot explains. The style of the scenery was influenced by traveling shows of the early 1900s, like Buffalo Bill's Wild West. They are deliberately theatrical, occasionally ripped, and not hung up too well. But there's no doubt that they are of the wizarding world: These images move!

MAGIZOOLOGY 101

As a Magizoologist, Newt Scamander has been traveling the world in search of creatures from the sweet and cuddly to the highly dangerous. Prop makers ensured that, in addition to Newt displaying hundreds of artifacts from his adventures, he had all the necessary equipment for his vocation—for example, a net with which to catch creatures and a scale with which to weigh them, which he keeps in a shed in his case. The props team also worked with the graphic department to create bottles to hold medicinal ingredients and sundries for grooming, such as Horn Polish, Beak Balm, and Shell Shiner. There's a stack of diaries in which Newt has written his observations, as well as books for reference, including the *Bestiarium Magicum*.

Being a caretaker for many animals, Newt needs to keep track of their meal schedules. So lead graphic designers Miraphora Mina and Eduardo Lima created a feeding dial. Classification, habitat, and feed codes are represented on a spinning wheel. Newt has written a list of creatures around his dial in alphabetical order. Turn the dial to a section and cut-outs reveal notes on classifications and needs. Tacked onto the dial are a sketch and a written reminder to "Remove all shiny objects during feeding of Niffler."

Magizoology Training

To research his role as a Magizoologist, actor Eddie Redmayne met with a variety of people in similar businesses: animal handlers, zookeepers, and other wildlife technicians and caretakers. "They all talked passionately about their techniques and their methods," recalls Eddie. He also went to safari parks and met with animal breeders. "They told me stories of the extraordinary relationships between the humans and animals," he says. "I could see how they really felt at one with the environment and celebrated nature."

BOWTRUCKLE

Bowtruckles are tree-dwelling creatures that resemble their habitat—they're like a walking ensemble of sticks and branches. Newt has a Bowtruckle named Pickett who likes to live behind his coat lapel. "Pickett may be my favorite character in the film," actor Eddie Redmayne declares. He describes Pickett as being a loner within his family of Bowtruckles who even feels a bit bullied by his friends. "He has attachment issues," Eddie says with a laugh. "So he keeps faking illnesses in order to keep hanging out in my coat." Bowtruckles are incredibly agile, and because Pickett can pick locks, he proves to be of great value to Newt in a time of need.

The Bowtruckle's Environment

Even though Pickett the Bowtruckle likes to hang out behind Newt's coat lapel, his environment within the case is a perfect place for his family and friends to live— though they'd be really hard to find among the tree branches!

THUNDERBIRD

One of the creatures in Newt's case is the Thunderbird, which he found in Egypt and has brought to America to return to its native Arizona home. "The Thunderbird's called Frank," Eddie says, "and Newt found him being trafficked there. He wants to bring Frank back to where he belongs and free him." Thunderbirds are legendary creatures. It is said that the beating of their enormous wings causes thunder and that lightning flashes from their beaks.

The Thunderbird's Environment

The Thunderbird's environment within Newt's case is Southwestern in feel, reflecting its Native American roots. On its plateau-like platform are saguaro cacti and some "balancing" red rocks (these kind are called "mushrooms" or "hats") you find scattered throughout the western states. Their shape is caused by water erosion—mostly from rainstorms!

THE ERUMPENT

The Erumpent is a prominent creature in *Fantastic Beasts and Where to Find Them*. Eddie Redmayne describes her as a mash-up of a rhinoceros and an elephant. "I love the Erumpent," he proclaims. "The Erumpent is fast and gigantic. And, during our story, there is a moment when the Erumpent is also looking for a mate!" In order to get the Erumpent back into the case, Newt has to entice her. "That may have involved one of the more humiliating moments in the film," Eddie confesses, "in which I had to do an Erumpent mating dance. It was weirdly exhausting trying to seduce an Erumpent—but also a massive high point." A wire cage, full-scale Erumpent was operated from the inside by a team of puppeteers that brought the creature's movements and personality to life.

Central Park Zoo

Newt's recovery of the Erumpent takes place at New York's Central Park Zoo, which didn't exist in 1926. Before there was a park, there was a medieval-style Arsenal. People started donating animals to it, and it became an official zoo in 1934. "So we cheated a bit," says production designer Stuart Craig. "But the buildings for our zoo are in a similar architectural style to the original Arsenal, so it feels and looks very much like that part of Central Park."

The Erumpent's Environment

One challenge for creating the Erumpent's environment was showing that she wasn't in it. Concept artist Dermot Power knew that the audience had to be able to quickly discern that this was an environment for a very large creature and also that something was missing. Concept art first shows the empty habitat and then the aftermath of the creature's escape. From the size of the hole and the broken slats, it's obvious that a huge animal was housed in there.

THE NIFFLER

One of the most fantastic—and funny—creatures is the Niffler. The Niffler appears to be a cross between an anteater (he's got a long snout) and a mole (he's a great digger) or a badger (with his long claws) and a wallaby (he's got a marsupial-type pouch) or . . . It's hard to describe what's going on beneath his fluffy black fur! Nifflers are cute and cuddly until they spot something that sparkles, which they then go after with unparalleled single-mindedness. "He's a cheeky, canny little fellow, and he's an agile one," says actor Eddie Redmayne. "This little thing manages to wind his way out of my case and wreak havoc. It all goes horribly, horribly wrong, and this one little catalyst sets in motion an insane amount of events that just cause chaos." Eddie says that Newt has a love/hate relationship with the Niffler: "But Newt can't help but love him a bit more despite the fact that he is endlessly causing him trouble."

THE SWOOPING EVIL

The Swooping Evil is perhaps the most mysterious creature of the lot. Newt Scamander is able to use this beautiful creature to help him when he's in trouble, so maybe the "evil" part of its name isn't quite right. The appearance of the Swooping Evil seems to take inspiration from both butterflies and bats. It rests in a cocoon covered in sharp protrusions. When Newt flings this encased version of the creature into the air, it opens and extends into a birdlike or batlike flying animal. The Swooping Evil's underside is a magnificent cobalt blue. Its skeletal structure can be seen through its thin wings, and its skeletal head resembles that of a rodent, with long, saber-shaped canine teeth. Good thing it's on Newt's side!

Taking Flight

Since the wizarding world was first seen on the movie screen, the most important creative rule for all the creatures has been that their anatomy and movement should be based on naturalism. The beasts in *Fantastic Beasts and Where to Find Them* are truly fantastic, but they are rooted in the realm of the possible. It takes a lot of research and drawings before an artist creates a piece of concept art that is then used by the visual effects team to develop even further until the final creature is approved by the director and producers. For creatures such as the Swooping Evil, the artists studied birds, bats, and even flying mammals to observe how their body structures as well as their feathers or fur would influence movement. Even though the fantastic beasts were created in an animated format, rules of biology and practicality were still applied. Equally important was the personality of each of the creatures. Creatures can be good or bad, smart or stupid, and expressing that was especially significant to illustrate the individual relationships that Newt Scamander has with them.

MAKE IT YOUR OWN

Before you start building and decorating your model, read through the included instruction sheet. Then, choose a theme and make a plan. Here is a sample project to get those creative juices flowing.

With its eerie luminescence, the Swooping Evil astounds all who are privileged enough—or, perhaps, not so privileged—to witness its appearance. Since decorating this model provides many opportunities to mix and blend colors, paints are an especially nice medium to use for this project.

WHAT YOU NEED	WHAT YOU MIGHT WANT
Paintbrush	Water-based gouache paint
Blue, black, lime green, and gray paint	Three shades of blue
	Two shades of gray
	Three shades of green

It's easier to build the Swooping Evil before you paint it. Paint the stand separately though, and then assemble when everything is dry.

BODY

1. After assembling the model without the stand, paint the front body—not the wings or head—black.

2. Paint the tails black.

3. Paint the skull light gray.

4. Paint the inside of the eyes black.

Gouache paint is a type of opaque watercolor. It blends nicely and coats the wood well. If you don't have gouache, acrylic paint will work as well.

Paint the stand solid black to show off the bright colors of the Swooping Evil.

1. Start by painting the inside of the engraving marks light blue.

2. Go back and paint the engraved lines dark blue. It's okay to make your painted lines thicker than the engraved lines.

3. Outline the wings and tail pieces in black. But make sure to leave the edges plain. Blend part of the black with the dark blue edging to create a gradient.

> **Go a step further:** Paint a medium shade of blue where the light blue and dark blue sections meet. Blend the colors to get a nice luminescent look.

BACK WINGS

1. Start by painting the back side and edges of the wings lime green.

2. Paint the spikes a lighter shade of lime green.

3. Dab dark green paint along the horizontal edges of the wing folds. Blend the dark green paint into the background. Using a medium green paint between the dark green and the background green will help.

4. Add lime green details to the tail.

> **Go a step further:** To add texture bumps, paint dots with a dark green color. Then add smaller light green dots on top of the darker dots.

IncrediBuilds™
A Division of Insight Editions LP
PO Box 3088
San Rafael, CA 94912
www.insighteditions.com

Find us on Facebook: www.facebook.com/InsightEditions
Follow us on Twitter: @insighteditions

Library of Congress Cataloging-in-Publication Data available.

ISBN: 978-1-68298-062-0

Publisher: Raoul Goff
Art Director: Chrissy Kwasnik
Designer: Leah Bloise
Executive Editor: Vanessa Lopez
Project Editor: Greg Solano
Associate Editor: Katie DeSandro
Production Editor: Elaine Ou
Production Manager: Thomas Chung
Production Coordinators: Sam Taylor and Leeana Diaz
Model Design: Ball Cheung, Team Green
Craft Sample: Jill Turney

INSIGHT EDITIONS would like to thank David Heyman, Victoria Selover,
Melanie Swartz, Elaine Piechowski, Margo Guffin, Kevin Morris, Jill Benscoter,
Niki Judd, Gina Cavalier, Kate Cellan-Jones, and Nick Gligor.

Insight Editions, in association with Roots of Peace, will plant two trees for each tree
used in the manufacturing of this book. Roots of Peace is an internationally renowned
humanitarian organization dedicated to eradicating land mines worldwide and
converting war-torn lands into productive farms and wildlife habitats. Roots of Peace
will plant two million fruit and nut trees in Afghanistan and provide farmers there
with the skills and support necessary for sustainable land use.

Manufactured in Shaoguan, China, by Insight Editions

10 9 8 7 6 5 4 3 2